The Hawk of the Castle

The Hawk
of the Castle

A STORY OF MEDIEVAL FALCONRY

DANNA SMITH

illustrated by
BAGRAM IBATOULLINE

CANDLEWICK PRESS

First edition 2017

Library of Congress Catalog Card Number pending
ISBN 978-0-7636-7992-7

17 18 19 20 21 22 CCP 10 9 8 7 6 5 4 3 2 1

Printed in Shenzhen, Guangdong, China

This book was typeset in Throhand Ink.
The illustrations were done in acrylic gouache.

Candlewick Press
99 Dover Street
Somerville, Massachusetts 02144

visit us at www.candlewick.com

To my father, Dale Kessimakis,
who taught me how to "fly"
D. S.

To my dearest friend Anastasia Chaadaeva
B. I.

This is me.
This is my father.
This is our home, the castle.

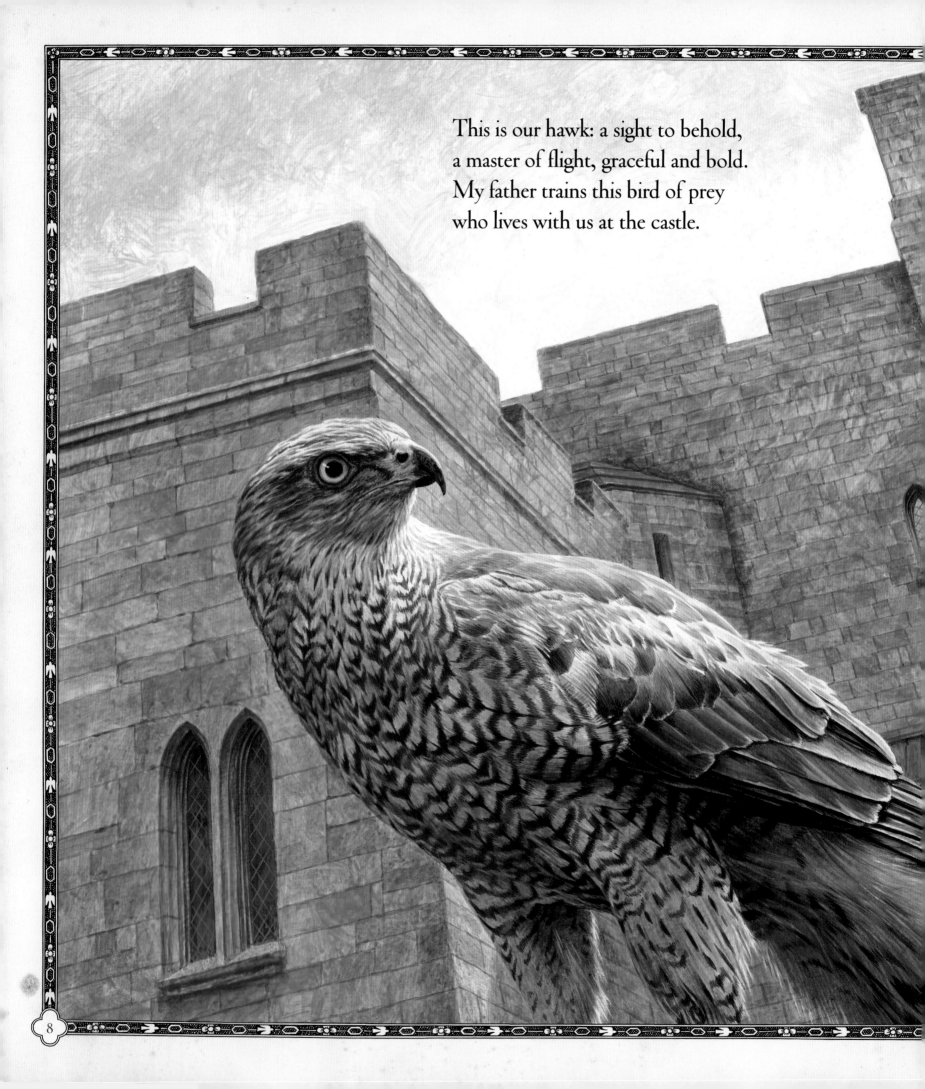

This is our hawk: a sight to behold,
a master of flight, graceful and bold.
My father trains this bird of prey
who lives with us at the castle.

A bird of prey, also called a raptor, is a bird that hunts animals such as ducks, pheasants, rabbits, grouse, and squirrels for food. Raptors have hooked beaks for tearing the meat they eat, dagger-like talons for grasping their prey, and excellent eyesight and hearing.

Since medieval times, people have hunted primarily with two kinds of raptors: hawks and falcons. Hawks have a rounded tail and short or broad wings, which allow them to fly more slowly and glide more often than falcons. Falcons, on the other hand, are built for speed, with a streamlined body, long tail, and long, pointed wings.

This is the perch our hawk likes the best,
a comfortable place that allows him to rest,
which he quietly grips while we prepare
for his flight outside the castle.

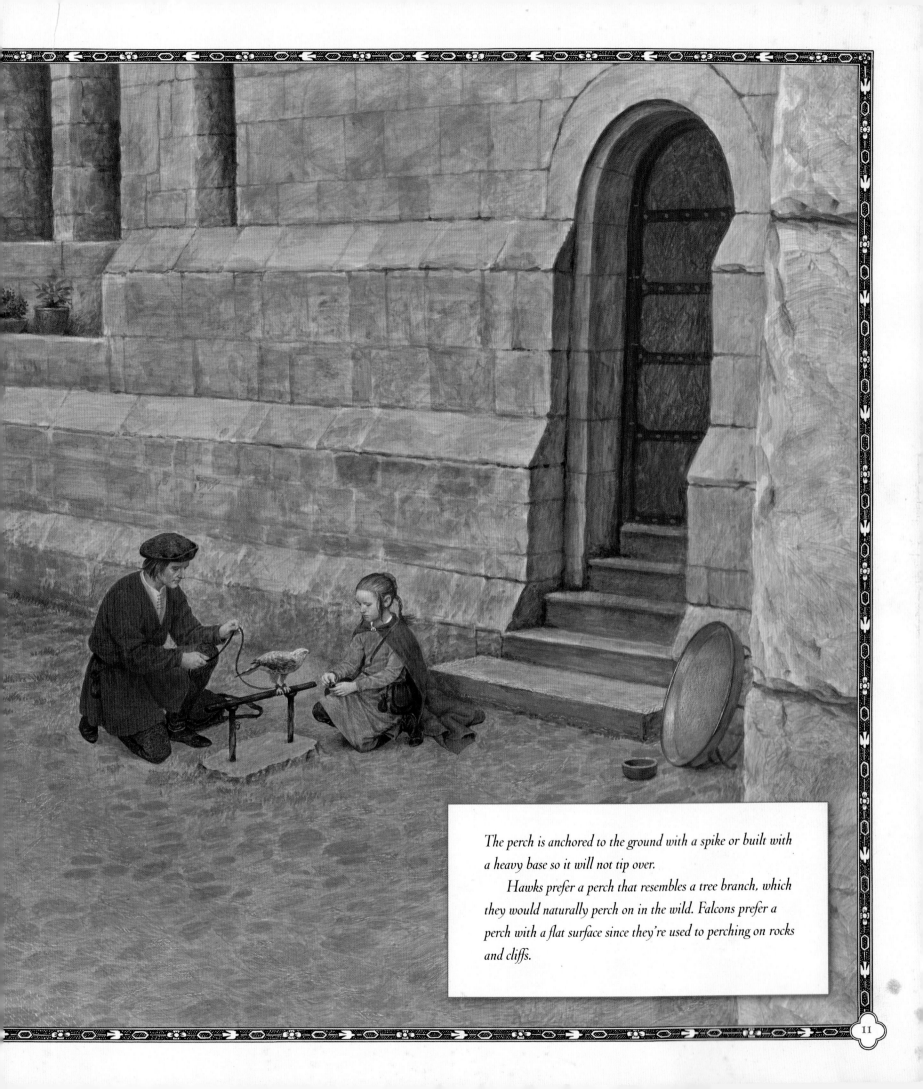

The perch is anchored to the ground with a spike or built with a heavy base so it will not tip over.

Hawks prefer a perch that resembles a tree branch, which they would naturally perch on in the wild. Falcons prefer a perch with a flat surface since they're used to perching on rocks and cliffs.

This is the glove with scratches and flaws
which protects Father's hand from razor-sharp claws
that grasp with ease and hold on tight
as we make our way from the castle.

Also called a gauntlet, a falconer's leather glove extends up
the arm for extra protection from the hawk's sharp claws.

This is the hood he wears on his head,
with fancy top feathers of purple and red.
It hides his eyes so he's not afraid
of soldiers who roam 'round the castle.

A hawk's hood is made of soft leather. It is slipped over the bird's head, covering its eyes to keep it calm. If the hawk sees something that frightens or interests it, it might react by trying to fly from the perch or the falconer's fist while tied to the leash. If a bird flaps its wings while tethered (also known as bating), it can damage its wings.

The fancy feathers on top are not only for decoration; they are also used as a handle when removing the hood.

The falconer trains not only his or her raptors but also the
hound that helps in the hunt. The perfect hunting spot is any
wide-open space with plenty of wild prey, or game.

This is the hound that we like to take
to a wide-open field that's down by the lake.
She is carefully trained to help us to hunt
for game with our hawk of the castle.

These are the bells attached to our bird
that jingle and ring so he can be heard.
We slowly remove the hood from his head;
now he's ready to hunt for the castle.

Bells are attached to the bird's legs to help the
falconer locate the bird after it's downed its prey.
The hawk flies and dives at such amazing speeds
that by the time the prey hears the bells, it has
little chance of escaping.

This is the arm Father raises just right
that signals our hawk when it's time to take flight.
With a stretch of his wings, he flies from the fist
and soars above the castle.

When it's time to hunt, the falconer will "throw the hawk off,"
quickly moving his or her arm forward to give the hawk a boost
into the air.

Falconers can become attached to their birds, but birds of prey are not pets and have no affection toward the falconer. The hawk allows the falconer to share in its hunt because it trusts that the falconer will feed and protect it.

This is the sky that's filled with the sound
that's made by our hawk and heard from the ground.
He opens his beak and calls to the wind.
It is music to us at the castle.

These are the grouse that fly in a rush
when flushed by our hound from under the brush.
Our hawk folds his wings and dives headfirst
in pursuit of his prey for the castle.

*Birds of prey can see eight times better than a human.
Sharp eyes are necessary when a hawk needs to spot
dinner from hundreds of feet up in the sky. To flush
prey means to drive it out into the open.*

24

These are his feet, a powerful pair
with talons that strike with force in midair.
He binds his prey and carries his catch
back down to the field by the castle.

A hawk's claws, or talons, allow the hawk to kill, grasp,
and carry heavy prey. The bird's rapid descent, or dive,
from the sky is called a stoop. After the hawk strikes, it
grabs and holds (binds) its quarry (the animal or bird
hunted by the hawk) to bring it down to the ground.

This is the grass as tall as can be,
which hides our hawk so he's hard to see.
We follow the sound of jingling bells
that leads to our hawk of the castle.

The bells ring as the raptor moves its feet while grasping the prey, alerting the falconer to its whereabouts in the tall grass or up in a tree. The sound carries best when two bells of different tones are used together.

If the bird does not catch its prey, a lure can be used to call it back to its master. A lure is a decoy, sometimes baited with raw meat. The falconer swings the lure over his or her head, then drops it to the ground as the bird swoops down to tackle it.

This is the dinner our hawk likes to eat,
which I place on my hand, right down at his feet.
He'll nibble his treat until he is full,
a reward for our hawk of the castle.

Falconers often keep their birds' catch for themselves, but treat
their hawks to a small bird or a few small pieces of game. Along
with meat, falconers sometimes let their birds eat a few feathers,
bones, or bits of fur, which the
bird throws up later. This is
called casting and helps
the bird digest its food.

This is the pan we fill to the brim,
round as the moon with a smooth silver rim
that holds the cool water that splashes on him
as the sun slowly sets on the castle.

A large shallow pan is filled with clean water and placed near the hawk's perch. The bird uses the water as it preens, grooming its feathers with its beak. Sometimes, if the hawk gets thirsty, it will sip the bathwater.

This is our sleepy bird ready for bed,
closing his eyes and tucking his head.
We wish him peace and bid him good night.
Sleep tight, our hawk of the castle.

A hawk lives in a house called a mews. A mews is
designed to keep a bird safely inside and its predators
outside. Built with windows for natural light and
ventilation, a mews is large enough for a hawk to move
freely inside without damaging its wings.

AUTHOR'S NOTE

My father was a falconer, so I was fortunate to learn about this ancient sport firsthand. I have wonderful memories of going out to "fly" with my dad. We would travel to the countryside on a cool, crisp fall day, and Dad would place a hawk on my fist. The bird weighed less than 900 grams (two pounds), but when held out to my side, it felt very heavy. Dad would tell me when it was time to throw the hawk off, and it was exhilarating to experience the hawk leaping into the sky. When it was just a tiny speck above us, Dad and I watched through binoculars. It always took my breath away to see Dad's hawks gliding on the wind. Falconry is an experience like none other.

Falconry dates back to China and the Middle East more than three thousand years ago. It became extremely popular in Europe in the Middle Ages, between 500 and 1500 CE. In medieval times, falconry was called the king's sport. History tells us of kings and lords who used falconry not only as a way of obtaining food but also as an opportunity to entertain other nobles by taking them on grand hunting parties. Well-trained birds of prey were valuable and therefore given as royal gifts, used as payment of debts, and offered as prizes for winning tournaments. Many castles housed falconers whose only job was to capture, train, and care for birds of prey so they would be ready to hunt with noblemen and their guests. Master falconers were paid very well for their expertise and were honored and admired for their skills. Under ancient laws, the thief of a trained bird of prey, its eggs, or newly hatched young would receive harsh punishment and sometimes even be put to death!

Kings and lords were not the only people to practice falconry. In *The Boke of Saint Albans*, published in 1486, author Dame Juliana Berners suggests that a person's rank in society dictate which species of bird he or she may use. The most prestigious raptors were eagles and vultures, which would be owned only by an emperor. Gyrfalcons were for kings; peregrines for princes, dukes, and earls; saker falcons for knights; merlin falcons for ladies; goshawks for yeomen; sparrow hawks for priests; all the way down to kestrels (small birds that catch small prey) for servants and children. Not everyone followed these guidelines, but owning a bird above your rank was seen by society as an act of rebellion.

The old ways of training and hunting with birds of prey have been passed down for centuries. Falconry has survived and thrived throughout the years, and there are falconry clubs and those who are working tirelessly to protect birds of prey around the world. With the invention of new technology, some equipment, products, and material used in falconry have changed; however, much of the time-honored ways of falconry remain, including the custom that specific birds be flown based on the different class or level of falconry experience one possesses. As in the past, some falconers today eat the game hunted by their birds, while others practice falconry for the sport only, allowing the bird to eat its quarry. A major concern of falconers today is that the ever-growing number of roads, power lines, and turbines are leading to the dwindling of safe, wide-open spaces to fly birds of prey.

Because raptors are protected by state, federal, and international law, all potential falconers must obtain permits and licenses before acquiring a hawk or practicing falconry. The process of becoming a licensed falconer differs by state and country and can take years. This process may include obtaining falconry sponsors, completing an apprenticeship, taking hunting classes, passing written exams, paying fees, and proving to officials that you have the facilities and the equipment necessary to keep a raptor.

By watching my father, I learned many things about falconry, but the most important things I learned are that falconry takes daily dedication and patience, and that birds of prey must always be treated with care and respect.

FOR FURTHER READING AND INFORMATION

BOOKS

Ap Evans, Humphrey. *Falconry.* New York: Arco, 1974.

Berners, Juliana. *The Boke of Saint Albans.* Saint Albans, England: Schoolmaster-Printer, 1486. London: Elliot Stock, 1881. Reprint, New York: Da Capo, 1969.

Macdonald, Fiona. Illustrated by Mark Bergin. *A Medieval Castle.* New York: Peter Bedrick, 1990.

McNeill, Sarah. *Medieval Places.* Brookfield, CT: Millbrook, 1992.

Oggin, Robin S. *The Kings & Their Hawks: Falconry in Medieval England.* New Haven: Yale University Press, 2004.

Parry-Jones, Jemima. *Training Birds of Prey.* Devon, England: David & Charles, 1994.

Samson, Jack. Illustrated by Victoria Blanchard. *Falconry Today.* New York: 1976.

WEBSITES

"Falconry and Hunting in the Middle Ages." Bright Hub Education. www.brighthubeducation.com/history-homework-help/107330-falconry-and-hunting-in-the-middle-ages/.

North American Falconers Association. www.n-a-f-a.com/.

The Falconry Centre. www.thefalconrycentre.co.uk/.

INDEX